It Grows in Spring

Learning the GR Sound

Autumn Leigh

Phonics
for the
REAL World™

Rosen Classroom Books and Materials™
New York

New plants grow from seeds in spring.

A grown-up can help you plant seeds in the ground.

Rain falls from gray clouds to help the seeds grow.

7

The sun helps seeds grow.

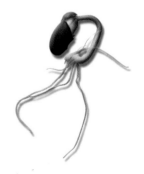

9

The seeds grow into small green plants.

The small green plants grow bigger.

13

The plants grow green leaves.

Some plants grow flowers.

Some plants grow food.

What other things grow in spring?

Word List

gray

green

ground

grow

grown-up

Instructional Guide

Note to Instructors:
One of the essential skills that enable a young child to read is the ability to associate letter-sound symbols and blend these sounds to form words. Phonics instruction can teach children a system that will help them decode unfamiliar words and, in turn, enhance their word-recognition skills. We offer a phonics-based series of books that are easy to read and understand. Each book pairs words and pictures that reinforce specific phonetic sounds in a logical sequence. Topics are based on curriculum goals appropriate for early readers in the areas of science, social studies, and health.

Letters/Sound: **gr** – Write **g** and **r** on a chalkboard or dry-erase board. Ask the child to blend these two sounds together to make the **gr** sound. Write several words that begin with **gr** on the chalkboard or dry-erase board and ask the child to decode them. (Word suggestions: *green, grass, grown-up, ground, grow, gray.*) Have them underline **gr** in each of the words and use them in sentences.
- Write the following words on the chalkboard or dry-erase board: *grandmother, goat, grape, go, grade, game, grandfather, gave.* Ask the child to read them and choose only those that begin with **gr**. Have the child underline **gr** in each of them.

Phonics Activities:
- Give the child a large flower made from construction paper that includes a stem, leaves, and a large circle placed on top of the stem. Provide patterns of flower petals for the child to color and cut out. Ask them to write **gr** on the leaves or stem of the flower and write a word on each petal. Instruct them to place the petals around the outside of the circle to form a flower. Have the child continue adding **gr** words so that their flower "grows."
- Ask the child to read their **gr** flowers to you. Review *It Grows in Spring.* Have the child name words and pictures in the story that begin with the following consonant blends: **pl**, **cl**, and **fl** *(plants, planting, clouds, flowers).* Have them name additional words beginning with these sounds and use them in sentences about spring.
- Give the child a **gr** card. Make up a simple story about gardens with several **gr** words in it. Ask the child to raise their **gr** card every time they hear a **gr** word.

Additional Resources:
- Fowler, Allan. *How Do You Know It's Spring?* Danbury, CT: Children's Press, 1991.
- Good, Elaine W. *That's What Happens When It's Spring.* Intercourse, PA: Good Books, 1995.

Published in 2002 by The Rosen Publishing Group, Inc.
29 East 21st Street, New York, NY 10010

Copyright © 2002 by The Rosen Publishing Group, Inc.

All rights reserved. No part of this book may be reproduced in any form without permission in writing from the publisher, except by a reviewer.

Book Design: Ron A. Churley

Photo Credits: Cover, pp. 11, 17, 21 © SuperStock; p. 3 © Pam Gardner/Frank Lane Picture Agency/Corbis; pp. 4, 6, 8, 10 © PhotoDisc; p. 5 © Myrleen Cate/Index Stock; p. 7 © Dario Perla/International Stock; pp. 9, 13 © Richard Hamilton Smith/Corbis; p. 15 © Mark E. Gibson/International Stock; p. 19 © Bob Firth/International Stock.

Library of Congress Cataloging-in-Publication Data

Leigh, Autumn, 1971-
  It grows in spring : learning the GR sound / Autumn Leigh.
      p. cm. — (Power phonics/phonics for the real world)
  ISBN 0-8239-5941-4 (library binding)
  ISBN 0-8239-8286-6 (pbk.)
  6-pack ISBN 0-8239-9254-3
  1. Growth (Plants)—Juvenile literature. 2. English
language—Consonants—Juvenile literature. [1. Growth (Plants)]
  I. Title. II. Series.
  QK731 .R69 2002
  571.8'2—dc21
                                                        2001019627

Manufactured in the United States of America